Dedicated to my husband Murray and my
Griffin for their love and support. I could not have done it
without you. You each inspire me everyday.
– ATJ

To my two families – my German one and my American one
because you support me in everything I do and
I am so thankful to have you.
– SS

Acknowledgments

To Jillian Michaels for the seeds in a conversation, to Peter Barnes for pointing out the rocks in the garden, to Melissa Mangano for hoeing the words by giving them a voice, to Dr. Jill Jordan McMillan and Janie Simms Hamner, MD for pulling the weeds by editing and to Toni Filipone and the entire Tampa Team for watering the project with encouragement.

Oh little one, I love you so.

I want you healthy as you grow.

Let's teach you how to care for yourself.

And to make good choices, my sweet little elf.

Healthy is a lifestyle, not a diet or a fad.

Healthy is how you were meant to be,
For that you should be glad.

Care for and love your body,
It's the only one you've got.

All the fun and active choices,
Will help you out a lot.

Oh little one, I love you so.

I want you playing as you grow.

Go hiking, go biking,
Try martial arts.

Be a dancer, be a runner,
With YOU is where it starts!

Go be silly at the park,
Swing from the monkey bars.

When you are out being active,
You are reaching for the stars.

Oh little one, I love you so.

I want you learning as you grow.

Eating right, staying active and
getting enough rest,

Will keep your mind and body
Working at their very best.

Life is full of choices, no matter what your age.

When you set a good example,
you soon take center stage.

When friends suggest just sitting down
and eating junkie food,

Jump up and say, "come on let's play"
it will put you in a great mood.

Calories in, calories out –
Oh, what does it really mean?

Eating right and exercising,
The changes will be seen...

Eating right and exercising make healthy kids
and parents, too.

While making the right choices,
change will be seen in YOU!

Oh, little one
I love you so.

I want to teach you
As you grow.

Eat apples to zucchini
And all letters in between —

Put a rainbow on your plate
Red, yellow, orange and green.

Never skip your breakfast, or your dinner,
or your lunch.

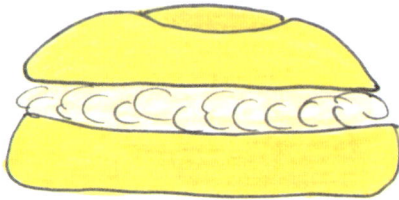

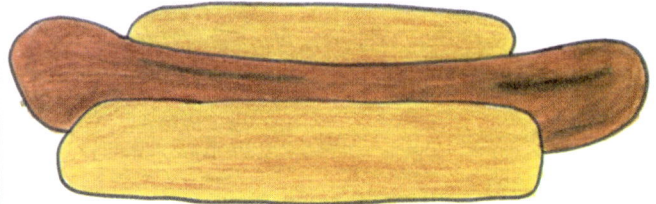

Even eat a snack each day,
Be balanced when you munch.

Cook a meal together, it's a way to learn a lot.

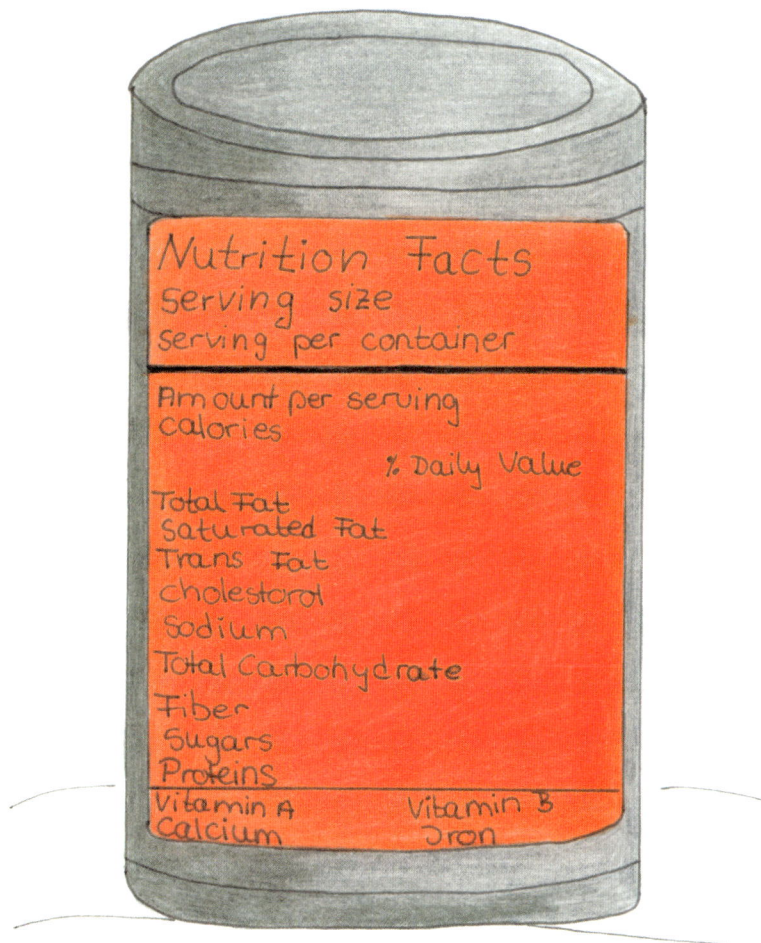

Nutrition Facts

Serving size
Serving per container

Amount per serving
Calories

% Daily Value

Total Fat
Saturated Fat
Trans Fat
Cholestorol
Sodium
Total Carbohydrate

Fiber
Sugars
Proteins
Vitamin A   Vitamin B
Calcium   Iron

About YOUR likes and dislikes,
and the nutrition that they've got.

When you plant a garden,
the seeds that you will sow.

Fresh fruits and vegetables,
for all is what you'll grow.

The world is full of healthy things
For you to eat and do.

Little one, your job for now
Is to find what's right for <u>YOU</u>.

Oh little one,
I love you so.

I want you healthy
As you grow.

To be the grown-up
You were meant to be —

Wise and strong
And living healthfully.

It is never too early to aim to be strong
Make healthful choices,

You will never go wrong!